9781572819962

PLAYING MARSEILLE

By Ryan Edward

Copyright © 2020 U.S. GAMES SYSTEMS, INC.

All rights reserved. The illustrations, cover design, and contents are protected by copyright. No part of this book may be reproduced in any form without permission in writing from the publisher, except by a reviewer who wishes to quote brief passages in connection with a review written for inclusion in a magazine, newspaper or website.

10　9　8　7　6　5　4　3　2　1

Made in China

Published by
U.S. GAMES SYSTEMS, INC.
179 Ludlow Street
Stamford, CT 06902 USA
www.usgamesinc.com

INTRODUCTION

Tarot cards are playing cards. In their original, most authentic form, they were designed for playing games. Created in the early 15th century during the Late Gothic period in Northern Italy, Tarot, Tarocchi, or Tarok was the first time the concept of trumps or trick-taking was introduced to card games. Bridge and all other games that involve a trump suit such as 'Spades' and 'Hearts' are derivatives of Tarot. This fun fact comes in handy during family game night.

Why is this important? Today there seems to be different classifications for how certain decks are meant to be read. Over the years, Tarot has gained so many layers of esoteric and psychological theory that it is considered a breed apart from the classic cartomancy of common playing cards and Lenormand decks. There are numerous different methods for reading cards. Many people have taken to these simple cartomantic decks because they are that, simple. They are free of the psychological, astrological, Kabbalistic, esoteric structure, making them clear and direct. What's important to remember is that these were all playing cards to begin with. We've applied different systems of reading onto them, but those divination systems are not inherent to the decks themselves.

TAROT
Typically a deck of 78 cards, with four suits of 10 pips + four courts each, with an added trump suit of 21 cards plus one Fool. Used for many trick-taking games.

"STANDARD" PLAYING CARDS
A similar deck as above, without the 5th suit of trumps, and only three court cards per suit. 52 cards in total. Used for a nearly endless number of card games.

THE PETIT LENORMAND
A reduced deck of 36 cards primarily used for a game called Jass. Again with four suits, but without numbers 2-5 (or without Ace, 3, 4, 5 in German packs). Also used for many trick-taking games. With added illustrations numbered 1-36, this became yet another game called *Das Spiel der Hoffnung* or "The Game of Hope" where certain good or bad cards and their suits lent to the fortune-telling functions of the cards.

There are some who may love to read playing cards, but shy away from reading the Marseille Tarot because "there's nothing on the pip cards." However, once you look at the Tarot as a playing card deck, then it all starts to make sense.

Playing Marseille works to make this correlation a bit

more evident. While not a true "Tarot de Marseille," this deck *plays* like one. When we think of playing cards we often think of a 52-card deck with the French suits; the red Hearts and Diamonds, and the black Clubs and Spades. Here, these have replaced the familiar Italian Tarot suits (Cups, Coins, Batons, and Swords), and blended with the classic Marseille pattern, which is a bit ironic considering the Marseille has always been a French deck.

This guidebook explains how to read the Tarot through the lens of classic playing card cartomancy. It focuses on straightforward, simple ways to interpret the cards, staying clear of esoteric approaches. You may adopt all of these methods, or choose which work best for you. The great thing about these decks without scenes on the Minor Arcana is that they are agnostic of any specific system. Our system is what we see in front of us; suits, colors, numbers and court cards. We examine lines, rhythms, and patterns. We look to see who's looking at whom. That's the brilliance of simple, basic methods; because they are so baseline, they can apply to many systems and types of cards. Take what you will and leave the rest, but hopefully you'll be able to learn a bit and have some fun in the process.

This is a humble, practical look at a tarot deck. And while you could look to a Lenormand or 52-card deck to provide simplicity, the Tarot is equally accessible. You just need to simplify the approach. But at the end of the day, this is just another Tarot deck, use it however you wish.

READING METHOD

The cards alone mean nothing. And any one card could mean a hundred different things. It's only when a series of cards are put in relation to each other, within the context and frame of the question, that a useful meaning surfaces. Think of the cards in action. Pay attention to what the cards are doing together before noting what any one card is. The Fool walks, the Magician tricks, and the Papesse keeps quiet. Series of pip cards can increase or decrease in number, patterns become rhythm, they develop a beat. Different cards with similar elements "rhyme." All together, it becomes melodic.

FIGURE CARDS
Both the trumps and court cards are our agents. They are our personifications of the concepts, themes, and people involved in the question. They act out the scenario in the most literal ways. We're not just interested in what is happening in each individual card, but what stories the cards tell by their position, gaze, and action in proximity and relation to one another.

COURT CARDS

To keep it simple and direct, these are our people in play. Courts of a suit are related by blood or association. Like squires, Pages/Jacks can represent the messages, and thus the thoughts, of the King or Queen of their suit.

TRUMP CARDS

These can also represent people, especially the first 9. But overall, the Trump cards can act out your answer for you. The action of the card may be more important than who that card is, if anyone. Together they become that much more dynamic.

POSITION

Our characters face left, right, or straight forward. Are two cards facing each other, or have their backs to one another? Is the Knight trying to get the Queen's attention with her back to him? If one card looks as if it's ignoring, or choosing another, it's because it is. We tend to think of the left as the past and the right as the future. Are cards dwelling on what was, or looking forward to what could be?

GAZE

The figure's position guides its gaze. Follow the line of sight. Is one card looking another in the eye, or are they focused on the Diamond instead? Is everybody facing the center? Look Justice in her (third) eye as she cuts to the truth.

ACTION

Cards can move swiftly, stand tall, or sit in waiting. Every card is doing something. Even the most still cards are not without action. The Hanged Man hangs, obviously. But his suspension, waiting to be released, is a far cry from the power of the Emperor, who sits while others do his bidding.

TRUMPS

LE FOL/THE FOOL walks. Hit the road, and don't come back. With his sack over his shoulder our Fool has left town, and he's on the move. In disheveled garb, it's safe to say he's not held in high regard. Has the animal torn down his pants. Or is he 'mooning' the animal? Is this animal his companion, or running him out of town? What is this animal anyway? It doesn't really matter. In your reading it may not be an animal at all, but something pestering you. I'd be more concerned how close it is to his nethers. His walking stick looks tired and grim, he's got a long walk ahead, as far as card XIII anyway.

I. LE BATELEUR/THE MAGICIAN tricks. He's got games to play, or is he playing you? Stay on your toes, this is a cunning one. Look at that shrewd glare. This is a classical street magician. He's here to swindle and gamble before packing his table up and moving to the next town. He's standing for now, but his time is temporary. He twirls his wand. With that hat and that coat, he's here to show off. Step right up if you're in for a bit of fun, but don't get hurt if you lose to this one.

II. LE PAPESSE/THE PRIESTESS stays silent. The library is closed, darling. Have a seat. She's got nothing to say to you. Fully clothed with barely any skin showing, this one knows a thing or two about discretion. Those who are silent, learn. She's learned much and continues to read up on more. Against a background of scrolls, very little is revealed in this card. She might be calm now, but she'll pop off when she's next to the Tower. She could be a doctor, scientist, lawyer, librarian, or witch. With all those arcane secrets, I wouldn't mess with this one.

III. L'IMPERATRIS/THE EMPRESS rules. She may be sitting still, but don't let that overshadow her agency. People come to her, not the other way around. She'll decide what do with them. With that side eye, it's clear she's not easily impressed. Look to the card on the right. Hopefully it pleases her. Motion pauses with this card, but it doesn't stop. There is no baby bump, child, or waves of grain. Using our practical methods, looking at the card, nothing here suggests fertility or motherhood. Maybe look to the Queen of Hearts for that. Can she be a mother? Sure, if the context relates. But the trump cards are gender fluid. The Empress can equally represent your father, again if the context calls for it.

IIII. LEMPEREUR/THE EMPEROR commands. With scepter stretched out, orders are had, word becomes law. This one's not playing around, until he is, then it's on his terms. His belt is held firm, highlighting the midsection, emphasizing the classic body language of the "macho man." Overcompensation is strong with this one. Like the Empress, he sits, but not without sway. His legs are crossed, square. Quite literally too, as they make the shape of the number 4—his number. This one is solid, he is braced. Best of luck getting past him easily.

V. LEPAPE /THE POPE directs. Either blessing or condemning, his hand motions forward. Priests are at his feet, he orders legions. He is the church. Many wars have been fought in the name of the gods. While the Emperor commands the army, the Pope commands them all. Look to the card to the right to follow his motion, his decree.

VI. LAMOUREU/LOVER chooses. Dazed and confused, our Lover is caught between two women. Old and young, they may be his mother and his lady friend. Laurels and flowers, they are virtue and vice. Should he stay or should he go? The age old question. It's all in the hands. They both reach for him. With a spaced out look of bewilderment, he puts his hands in precarious spots. He holds onto his belt, and reaches down for our young lady, perhaps out of impulse. This is the moment our blind Cupid strikes, the fireworks have gone off. There is choice, but no discernment. Practically speaking, this center figure is bombarded from all directions. This could be the center of attention, or a crippling bit of social anxiety depending on surrounding cards. The Lover makes a clear centerpoint if it falls in the middle of a string of cards. There are two opposing scenarios, I'd bet on the right.

VII. LE CHARIOR/THE CHARIOT drives. Full of pomp, this one. That hand on his hip, the other holding his tuliped scepter. He doesn't even have reins to hold. The horses are doing the work here, to their chagrin. But he'll get to where he wants to be, and he'll look good doing it. Good thing he's in the shade. Perhaps he's just won a war and is returning as the conquering hero. A common inference, considering Tarot's connection to Italian 'triumphi' victory parades. But look to the surrounding cards to fill in the story. Is our driver a hero, a charletan, or a parent dropping the kids off at soccer? Look to the most basic level first, then drive it from there.

VIII. JUSTICE cuts. Straight to the truth, there's no conning this one. That smirk, raised eyebrow, third eye, she knows precisely what's up. Her scales are aligned. Staring you in the face, this card is that of an instant. The swoosh of the sword, now an upright exclamation point, it all stands at attention. The law acts swiftly. Did she sentence XII to hang? With scales in hand and the rope around her neck, she may just be judge, jury, and executioner. Do not even try her.

VIIII. LERMITE/THE HERMIT gazes. Robed and staffed, he shines a light to the past. He stands in review, of what was, and still is. In older decks this was Father Time, holding an hourglass. But we don't see that in front of us. What we do see is a hunched back and a gray beard. So time and age are still implied in this card, maybe not as overtly. To function, the Hermit looks back. If he follows the Star, this could be a voyeur situation. If he follows the Sun, he could be reminiscing about childhood. If he begins a line of cards, pull another card to his left. It's important to know what he knows, or at least how he remembers it.

X. LA ROUE DE FORTUN/WHEEL OF FORTUNE spins. Time is a flat circle, and every season has its turn. It's all a matter of cycles. History repeats. We have our highs and lows. It's all by chance, and yet predictable at the same time. This is how fortunes are told. The only constant is change, after all. Our crowned figure is on top, but not for long. Are we focused on the creature ascending, or the robed figure descending? Look to neighboring cards to find the figures that rhyme. There's motion, but little progress. Situations can get caught in a loop here. The handle goes out of frame, left for the fates to spin, or the card to the right.

XI. FORCE/STRENGTH handles. She's got this. Caped and crowned, she's the superhero of the deck. A virtue to herself. Is she there to shut the lion up, or get it to open up? Look to the other cards. If this is to the left of VIIII, the Hermit might be inspecting what the lion has to say. Or, maybe this cat just has a furball, context dictating. Next to the Fool, the small thing pestering you might be a bit more problematic now. Whatever it is, Strength has it under control.

XII. LE PANDU/THE HANGED MAN hangs. Very little agency is left here. Their hands are up, or are they down? It's all about uncertainty. No idea, no control, no progress, at least with this card alone. A sharp blade, usually meant to hurt, would be this one's sweet release. Is Justice there to string them up, or cut them down? Follow the line of cards to find out how our hanged one fares. Right now they are waiting, not out of anticipation, but out of patience. That's all they can control, their response. Hang tight, take a breath, and someone will be along shortly.

XIII swipes. A figure has no name, only a scythe. The harvest has come. Death is implicit. The soil is rich and black, the bodies are ripe limbs for the picking, peasant or crown. Take what you will. It's time to leave like the Fool, the card with no number. Déjà vu sets in. Pay attention to these two if they fall in a string. The cards between will tell how one begets the other. That's as much "transformation" as you'll get with this one. If this card ends a string, don't expect a third act. The line is over, the answer is clear cut. Its freedom is absolute.

XIIII. TEMPERANCE blends. This is the alchemist. Carefully and methodically she blends. So skilled, she makes it look easy, mixing at an impossible angle without even looking. Standing tall, tonic swirls and twirls, blending in and out of her robes. Even the landscape flows, everything is fluid here. What are in the two jars? Look to the other cards to see what rhymes. Maybe they are the two beasts in the Moon, or the minions of the Devil, or the Pope's. Everything in moderation, perfect proportion, the final formula. They'll either regain balance, or fall by the wayside.

XV. LE DIABLE/THE DEVIL binds. A curious greeting from an even more curious figure. Wings spread wide, tuliped scepter raised, arm up. Has it been caught red handed, or is it you? It's not looking at anybody else at the moment. This card's ill comfort is that of corporal chaos. The blank stare, the tongue out, the smirk of the belly, the sleepy knees. All eyes on you. Its function is to bind. And the two bound imps are not here for it. Their displeasure is their dignity. Their faces say it all. If they follow the Sun, childhood may have ended. In the reverse, freedom awaits.

XVI. LA MAISON DIEU/THE TOWER disrupts. Chaos continues. While the tower still stands, the two figures fall. Blue flames knock off the crown. Did they rain from above, or explode from within? Are those dots stars, embers, fireworks, disco lights, confetti, or brimstone? Context dictates it all. There is one constant with this card however, and that is change. Whether disastrous or fun, things have been shook, they're not what they were, the status quo is obsolete. This card could represent a party as much as it could an accident. Perhaps an auto accident with the Chariot. If followed by the Priestess, her crown is put back on, her wig is fixed, and there's nothing to speak of.

XVII. LE TOILLE/THE STAR releases.
There's nothing left. No clothes, buildings, or possessions. There are only the two cups, which she happens to be pouring out. She has let it go. Minimalism at its finest. This card is a sharp contrast to Temperance. Restraint, method, and modesty are now countered by freedom, improvisation, and progression. Then again, Temperance could be mixing drinks, while the Star could represent sobriety. Context dictates. It's all relative. Follow these two if they fall together in a string. Their order should say much about the status of things.

XVIII. LA LUNE/THE MOON distorts.
Darkness falls, creatures howl and come from the depths. The tone is eerie. The people have gone. Things aren't always what they seem. We've lost the clarity of daylight. All that remains is the glow of the moon. Things are seen in a new light. But which is reality? Pay attention to the two beasts. Were they once the two horses of the Chariot, or the two Priests from the

Pope? Do they become the two children of the Sun? Look to see how these two rhyme. Maybe friend becomes foe. I hope you're not afraid of the dark.

XVIIII. LESOLEIL/THE SUN shines. Here comes the Sun. Dawn breaks. Darkness has been overcome. Of all the cards that came before it, the Sun dominates them all. It is our source, it gives us life. Even death has no purpose without it. Our childlike figures touch, skin to skin. They show intimacy, friendship, love. When rhyming with twos, it's always a delight to see these two end the string. Things have been made right. The Sun is pleased. Luck is on their side.

XX. LEIUGEMENT/JUDGMENT calls. The Angel's trumpet blares and the dead rise from their graves. The end has come, it's judgment day. Like the Moon and Sun that preceded it, the Angel of Judgment faces you head on, but shines with even greater radiance. There's no avoiding its call. Practically speaking, this is all calls, from invitations to text messages, to the morning alarm. Our figures, most likely a family, have received God's call. They're waking up. Or perhaps giving a standing ovation, after all this is our only musician in the deck. And the rapture is the ultimate encore.

XXI. LEMONDE/THE WORLD arrives.

The sky has parted. Heaven has come to Earth. The World is complete. This card has been represented by the new Jerusalem, the second coming of Christ, or Sophia his bride. A quincux, four figures with a fifth in the center, the quintessence, or fifth element. With Jesus at the center this is known as "Christ in Majesty" with these same four figures representing Matthew, Mark, Luke and John who spread the gospel to the four corners of the world. Here our figure is maybe more gender fluid, they can represent either or both at the same time. This card is blended essence. Practically speaking this is another person surrounded by others, even more so than the Lovers. The center of attention. This is also a card of borders, doorways, and liminal spaces. It is completion personified. Nothing trumps it. Fin.

RED & BLACK

COLOR

Our response to color is one of our most visceral reactions. The standard playing deck is classically known for being split into two colors, red and black. This also holds true for Tarot decks where coins and cups are bright yellow or gold suits, and the batons and swords are mostly black. Even the esoteric structure uses this same division to label them as feminine or masculine suits. This divide, while used popularly in French suited playing cards, also occurs in the Tarot deck with traditional Italian suits.

With 52 weeks, broken into four seasons of 13 weeks each, many say the classic playing deck is a representation of our year. If so, we would naturally look to red suits for the warm, bright half of the year, spring and summer. Conversely, the black suits represent the cold, dark half of autumn and winter. This gives us a natural dichotomy to the deck. Many suggest red is good and black is bad. While this may prove true in many contexts, do not make this a hard rule. If you're looking for work, many black Clubs could be a good thing. It is still important to note if one color is dominant, but think more in terms of purpose, energy, temperature, and season.

SUIT

We take the split of red/black one step further and analyze the four suits. With our metaphor of seasons, Diamonds kick off spring, followed by Hearts in summer. Autumn is in the Clubs while winter is with the dark, cold Spades.

Diamonds are our money and ideas. Cash burns a hole in our pocket if it's not already in our hot little hands. Our brightest minds are also our smartest. If we were to think in elements, Diamonds would be fire. In modern terms, this also translates to electricity and technology. This is the suit we find wealth, both of value and knowledge.

Hearts are our passions and loved ones. Our hearts beat. They pump blood through our body, which also runs through our family's. Represented by Cups in Italian suits, we raise a glass to this suit. This is only fitting considering we drink with our family and loved ones. Because of this, Hearts represent the element of water. Cheers!

Clubs bring people together through work or social gatherings. They provide the foundations of teamwork. We build together. They are the tools we work with, and woods we camp in. Clubs can represent wooden things, but their element is Air. Trees grow high in the sky and blow in the wind, while putting on a show in autumn.

Spades cut, stab, and dig. Even words can kill with a sharp tongue. Spades pierce both our enemies and the ground. We'll dig to plant a garden, or bury a body. They are the element of Earth. They are the razor edge of a craftsman's blade. This dark suit keeps secrets, it can be the arcane, occult, or good old practical magic.

COURTS

JACKS

The Jacks kickstart each suit of Courts. Each representing their respective season, if you look at the placement of their suns. They can represent the totality of their suit. They are the banner men, the messengers, a representation of their house. Then again, they could just be some kids, young adults if you will. Like everything thus far, we first mostly focus on their position, gaze, and function.

The Jack of Diamonds appraises. Their eye is sharp, and taste, discerning. It's hard for their gaze to extend the borders of the card, they are fixated on one thing, as is the pup. There's desire, with a hint of critique. Their smirk is mirrored by the spring sun. Things are new, ideas are fresh, their wit is sharp. Who else are they trying to lure with their wealth?

Serving some *contrapposto* with a switch in their hips, they are here to show off.

The Jack of Hearts follows. Like a horse with a carrot, or a lamb to the slaughterer, their path is set. Their sight is set on one thing. The first of the two "one-eyed Jacks" this one can't see beyond what's in front of them. At arm's length, their cup is stretched outward, cloaked by the heart on their sleeve. Follow the heart. The summer sun sets high on this one, full of surprise and delight.

The Jack of Clubs presents. That's a mighty big stick they have there. See if it moves throughout the string of cards. Next to the Ace of Clubs, there's a handoff of power. Regardless, the Jack wants to show it off, especially to the card on the right. Meanwhile, the setting autumn sun has a show all its own.

The Jack of Spades guards. The sword is drawn, teeth are clinched, and gaze is narrowed. This other one-eyed Jack sets his sight in the opposite direction. He is far less gullible, and far more alert. Even the low winter sun has their doubts. This Jack is ready to go toe-to-toe with the card on their right. Look to the following cards to see how it plays out.

KNIGHTS

The Knights are somewhat unique, especially in a playing card deck. As playing cards evolved over the years, court cards have come and gone. The Knights have been retained in the traditional Tarot pack, but did not make it into the common 52-card pack (which adds to the idea that the 52 count could be quite intentional). They are the people that fall between youth and seniority, full of agency, but short on power. The Knights are here to protect and serve their ruling King and Queen.

The Knight of Diamonds advances. Follow the money. Look to the cards on the left to find the source. The endgame is clear with this one. Even the Knight has their curious doubts, with a smirk of possible delight. Their horse advances slowly with only one hoof off the ground. Rushing will get them nowhere.

The Knight of Hearts lends. With an arm outstretched, offers are made and gifts bestowed. Their heart is out there, wide open, present and vulnerable. Look to the card on the left to see how it's received. The tilt of the Knight's head indicates that even they are not too certain. But that's probably part and parcel to putting yourself out there.

The Knight of Clubs extends. Here to reach out, or pass on, this Knight offers a helping hand, if the following cards play along. They may also play the antagonist, or perhaps the catalyst next to the explosive LA MAISON DIEU. Regardless, their expression seems genuine, but clearly the horse has doubts.

The Knight of Spades charges. Reservations aside, it's time to rush forward. Fully armored with sword drawn, this Knight is not playing around. Their horse is ready to charge, while the epaulette of moon is geared to watch the rear. It'll be hard to get to this one, skepticism at its finest. Look to nearby cards to see if they are leading a charge or defending their ground. Either way, the sequence is certain to become more dynamic with this one in the mix.

QUEENS

Enter our Grand Dames, mothers of their houses, matriarchs of their suits. These are the adult women of the deck, who appear in all corners of life. While they may fall second to their Kings in the order of the deck, don't underestimate their autonomy. In a string of cards they hold just as much influence. And in some cases, are far more balanced than their counterparts. I'm looking at you, Hearts.

The Queen of Diamonds flaunts. Look at her diamond. She can't keep her eyes off it. And neither should you. Whether it's the value of possession or mind, she wants you to know what she has. This goes beyond materialism. This is about owning what one has, and putting it out there for others to see, and maybe covet. She's here to show, but also share. Look to the left to find out how the transaction transpires.

The Queen of Hearts nurtures. Call her mother. As the matriarch of the suit of family, breasts exposed, she is here to take care of and watch over her cup. Unique to all the others, her cup is fully enclosed. Even she raises her eyebrows, curious to what's inside. Follow the string to see if and how that cup evolves.

The Queen of Clubs rests. Her poise is absent and her eyelids lowered. The sigh is nearly audible. The work has been done. Laurels abound. She is over it. Her slouch shows her indifference. Please, give her something of excitement or challenge. Even her elegant baton appears to be a bother. Meh.

The Queen of Spades anticipates. She is always two steps ahead, this one. The thorn on that flower won't compare to the one behind her back. With Spades at the end of the deck, her wisdom is in her experience as much as her age. She knows how to present herself as well as defend herself. Cutting.

KINGS

Men. Our fathers, grandfathers, bosses, and rulers, as a set they represent the antiquated notion of masculine superiority. But for our purposes, they are simply adult men. While they all sit, their nuance is in their gestures and gazes. Their reactions reveal their intentions.

The King of Diamonds possesses. Money falling into his palm, he only needs to reach out. Good thing he has two, because his left hand is full. Poised and refined with legs crossed, and robes flowing with style, this King is on point. But it is more than material, it's also cerebral. It takes wit and foresight to be in front of things, and have things come to you.

The King of Hearts tries. Bless his heart. He's doing all he can. His hands are full…all four of them. There's a need for more focus, less fluster. Passion can really have a way of scattering us. As per playing card tradition, this suicide king's blade is behind his head. Perhaps he's itching a scratch, downright careless, or maybe desperation has finally hit. Let the cards and context fill in the gaps.

The King of Clubs manages. He holds power in his right hand and a scepter, which also resembles a pen, in his left. He's here to lead and guide. Accountability is not lost on this one. With Clubs as the suit of work and people, our King is here to guide it all.

The King of Spades challenges. Proceed carefully, this King is quite capable of evisceration by way of words, law, or blade; all which fall under the suit of Spades. That is, if his eyes don't pierce first. The card on the right is in the most precarious position. Do they come in war or peace? It's best to be on this one's good side.

PIPS

PIP CARDS

These 40 cards, of four suits, in two colors, each Ace through ten are like notes. Each with their own beat, they add melody and rhythm to the deck. They flow and can bring nuance to the actions happening in the figure cards, or they can stand alone, giving the most clear and direct answers. Their elegance is in their simplicity.

FLOW

Before anything we look to see how the numbers progress. They'll either go up, down, bounce around, or we'll get multiple of a kind. A reading about money that descends from ten to two of Diamonds would be far less fruitful than a reverse string ending in the ten. Very little interpretation is needed. If the numbers bounce around, the situation may be more chaotic. Strings of a single number highlights that number's voice in the interpretation.

NUMBERS

Besides the flow of numbers, we can look at how each card is an intersection of suit and number. This information can add very specific and practical definition to a reading. Based on simple logic and the arrangement of the suit symbols, we can devise a function to each number 1-10 to blend with the meaning of the suit. This has sometimes been called the "heydgewytch" or "cunning folk" method. And while it can be infinitely useful, it is imperative for these interpretations to be considered subordinate to the flow and position. These are only here to add nuance to each reading, not to create whole meanings.

We'll delve into each of the 40 cards in a bit, but for now let's look at the numbers like this:

1. Beginnings
2. Exchanges
3. Growth
4. Security
5. Physical
6. Paths
7. Discontent
8. Collectives
9. Changes
10. Endings

ACE ⁕ BEGINNINGS

The Aces kickstart their suit. They hold the least in quantity but most in presentation. They're unique unto their own. And for that reason, they often carry with them their own unique traditions. But as a number, they are singular. Alone.

Ace of Diamonds: A single coin, a little money. With fire, a single flame. Traditionally, this card can represent a letter, especially when looked at lengthwise with the Diamond serving as a seal.

Ace of Hearts: A single drink, a little love, a small passion, a lonely heart. Traditionally, this card can also stand for the home, that is where the heart is after all. This plays well with the Marseille illustration of the castle-like structure.

Ace of Clubs: A single stick, an opportunity to build. A small chore, the first nail, a new job. Grab the baton and move forward. Take the torch, now find a light.

Ace of Spades: How infamous. This is a single stab, but it only takes one. Death is synonymous with this card. At one time in history, there was a sin tax placed on this card. Quite steep too. Forgery of it was punishable by death, and at least one forger paid that price.

TWO ⚜ EXCHANGES

A conversation. Exchanges occur in this set. Coins are transacted and cups are shared. Swords cross and battle lines are drawn.

Two of Diamonds: Money is exchanged. Deals are struck. Letters are swapped, invitations had, emails sent.

Two of Hearts: Cheers. One cup finds another. Maybe a first date. Harmony is sound.

Two of Clubs: A handshake, the first meet and greet between two people. Cooperation. Or perhaps some friendly competition.

Two of Spades: A duel. Cutting words are exchanged. Swords are crossed.

THREE ⁕ GROWTH AND LOSS

Two become three. Growth occurs. Hopefully it's benign.

Three of Diamonds: A spark. Ideas become interests. Money increases, perhaps a side paycheck or a small investment.

Three of Hearts: Joy. There's beauty here. Love grows. Three's a crowd, but not when drinks are involved.

Three of Clubs: Trees sprout. Work increases. Maybe a part-time job or some freelance work. Things begin to build and take shape.

Three of Spades: More cuts. Perhaps the work of a skilled craftsman, or someone with malintent. A little poison goes a long way. Even loss has a way of spreading.

FOUR ⚜ SECURITY

Four walls secure us inside. Each of these cards has four sides, literally and figuratively. In daily life, they represent four-sided things.

Four of Diamonds: A bank to hold our money, and a check to cash it. Or a ticket to pay. With fire, a hearth or a vehicle. With electricity, a monitor, tablet, or phone.

Four of Hearts: The bed, the couch. What happens within four walls. Families huddle close. Comfort is had here.

Four of Clubs: Offices, tables, desks, work. At least a bit of job security isn't a bad thing.

Four of Spades: The hole is dug, the grave is set. The sickbed awaits, thankfully it's not the final one. Lose the insecurity already.

FIVE ↔ THE PHYSICAL

What we experience with our body or hold in our hand.

Five of Diamonds: Pure energy. Fire itself. Here to cook a hot meal and nourish the body. Vitality.

Five of Hearts: Pleasure incarnate. Sex and swoon. Lust away. Enjoy it fully.

Five of Clubs: Physical work. Exercise. Manual labor. Get busy. There are things to build.

Five of Spades: Illness and pain. A sword to the gut.

SIX ~ TO AND FRO

Straight vectors. Two rows of three create a path. Using the binary color method, red may move forward while black recedes. They are clear and direct. Discerning by default.

Six of Diamonds: Roads and currents, sending electricity and communication. Information, money, and energy move from point A towards point B.

Six of Hearts: Pleasure seeking. Family trips. This card follows passion. Move forward towards what makes the heart beat.

Six of Clubs: Research. Going back to the people, work, and studies from before. Finding what was in order to move forward what is.

Six of Spades: Quit. Retreat. Back out.

SEVEN ⚜ DISCONTENT

The arrangement of the sevens in the playing card deck are the most unsettling. All the other odd numbers have a suit symbol dead center, but the seven has it inexplicitly at the top. It feel imbalanced, it calls for order. Something's not quite right.

Seven of Diamonds: Financial woes, the books are not balanced. Energy gone haywire.

Seven of Hearts: Heartache. The discontent of passion that wrenches the heart of an artist. The unsettling feeling of intuition.

Seven of Clubs: Things are faulty. Work needs done. Time to rebuild.

Seven of Spades: Failure and tears.

EIGHT ∞ COLLECTIVES

Groups of people and thoughts. This can be certain social circles, depending on the suit. Alternatively, they can represent collectives of thoughts bouncing around one head, or many.

Eight of Diamonds: Media and celebrity, the rich and famous. This card sparkles. Television and movies. Social media as a whole. Groupthink and networking thrive here.

Eight of Hearts: Party. The family is together for a feast, or the friends are over for some drinks. Although the two aren't mutually exclusive. Group hug.

Eight of Clubs: The team is together to go over the plans. Lecture is in session. Work meetings abound. Practical strategy. Clubs, literally. Like, the ones you join. Also the public, society itself.

Eight of Spades: Secrets. Selective societies, clandestine or otherwise. This could be a cloister of nuns, a fraternity house, the Masons, or the friendly neighborhood coven, context allowing. Sad gatherings, funerals and Shivas.

NINE ⁌ CHANGES

Things are about to shift. We've hit the end of single digits, evolution is around the corner. Buckle up.

Nine of Diamonds: Financial change, or shifting ideas. Look to the right to see how it ends.

Nine of Hearts: A change of heart. Traditionally, this is also the famous "wish card" to see where the heart lies. After all, a wish is simply a hope that things will change.

Nine of Clubs: A change of work or social status. Hopefully for the better; look to the other cards.

Nine of Spades: A painful change. Injury. Although sometimes the most painful changes are the most fruitful.

TEN ~ ENDINGS

Tens across the board, they are the destination. Which is why traditionally, two or more tens would indicate travel. Each is the epitome of their suit. While the Aces are a little, the ten is a lot. Often too much.

Ten of Diamonds: Total wealth, all of it, money and knowledge. Probably the suit in which you can't have 'too much.' Genius.

Ten of Hearts: Absolute bliss. Emotional high.

Ten of Clubs: Busy, overloaded. Dense woods and heavy crowds.

Ten of Spades: Worry and war. Demolition and decimation. Utter darkness.

READINGS

THREE CARD EXAMPLES

How should I proceed with my business?

Join another. Share the business with a partner. Together you will shine the brightest.

Why isn't he as available as before?

He was moving too fast before and got caught up between a few people. This has him at a stand still, not able to move forward.

Will the finances improve?

No. Despite the Diamonds at the end of the string, two is half of four. There will be a reduction of money on account of another.

Will he land the job?

Yes. The new job is his, but it's not what either of you know it to be.

How can I get over my dating hump?

Put your defenses all the way down, let them go. Be bare and vulnerable. Then your heart will point the direction.

FRENCH CROSS

The French Cross is a quintessential positional spread traditionally used with the Tarot de Marseille. Often it is used with just the Trumps, but we will explore this two ways. Its beauty is a combination of simple positions that still allow the cards to interact.

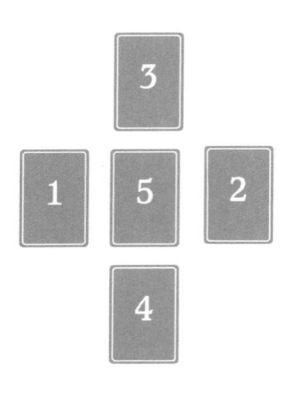

1: The situation or person in question
2: What card 1 faces, opposes, or interacts
3: Advice
4: Outcome
5: Quintessence *or tone of the overall reading*

Where do I stand with him? (Trumps only)

You sit (Emperor) in the past memory of the Hermit. It's time to find closure and move on (The World). There is no unification in this outcome (The Tower). This is an ending (XIII).

Is it worth my interest to pursue this new project?
(Full deck)

This joy (3 of Hearts) has awakened something in you (Judgment). If you're able to manage all the work (10 of Clubs) this will be well worth it, just what you've wanted (9 of Hearts). Follow your passion (Knight of Hearts), and give part of yourself to it.

NINE CARD EXAMPLE

The nine-card square is a staple in classic cartomancy with many decks. Take time to look at each row and column, followed by the diagonals. The bottom-right card being the last, and closest to the "outcome" paying particular notice to the influence of the card directly above it, while the center card is at the core of the reading. We want to pay attention to these steps, but it's still crucial to look at the spread holistically. That is your answer.

Would it be wise to plan a last minute trip to a Italy?
Not right now. If you pull the trigger out of impulse, you may likely have some regrets. We see a dance among our Jacks. Our Jack of Clubs starts at top, following joy. Moving one step forward, the Jack of Spades moves towards travel. But then a total aboutface, with our Jack of Hearts moving in the opposite direction after seeing 1 Diamond turn into five. Getting the paper ticket is easy, but the other costs may become intimidating. We see this exemplified in the final column. Our 2 of Spades in the final spot crowned with the Chariot and Wheel of Fortune suggests revisiting this another time. This trip (Chariot) is a clear 'no' (2 of Spades), but give it another cycle, another year (Wheel).

-53-

About the Creator

Ryan Edward is an artist from St. Louis, MO where he plays in the crossroads of design and magic in his studio. He is also the creator of Maybe Lenormand, the sister deck to Playing Marseille.

NOTES

For our complete line of tarot decks,
books, meditation cards, oracle sets,
and other inspirational products
please visit our website:
www.usgamesinc.com

Follow us on:

U.S. GAMES SYSTEMS, INC.
179 Ludlow Street
Stamford, CT 06902 USA
Phone: 203-353-8400
Order Desk: 800-544-2637
FAX: 203-353-8431